2

THE CHALLENGE OF THE
PRESENT CRISIS

THE CHALLENGE
OF THE
PRESENT CRISIS

HARRY EMERSON FOSDICK
*Author of "The Meaning of Prayer," "The Manhood of
the Master," etc.*

ASSOCIATION PRESS
124 EAST 28TH STREET, NEW YORK
1918

PRINTED IN THE UNITED STATES OF AMERICA

THE AUTHOR'S FOREWORD

I did not intend to write an essay on the War, and I am glad to see that I have avoided doing so. Many informing treatises are throwing light on every aspect of the great struggle, and it is not likely that there will be lack of more. But when all the special treatises have had their say, an inner problem still remains unsolved. In what mood shall a Christian, or for that matter an idealist of any kind, face the catastrophe? With what considerations and insights can he support his faith and hope? And how can he harmonize his ideals with his necessities of action in a time of war? The *morale* of our people critically depends upon their answer to such questions.

If one attempts to write upon the War with these needs in mind, the result cannot be an impersonal treatise. One must say out what his own thought has done in adjusting life to the strange and hor-

v

rible events of these days; he must plead
for the attitudes that seem essential to
the saving of man's spiritual treasures.
This little book, therefore, is a message,
not an essay, and while the pronoun of
the first person is absent, the background
of the argument is none the less the
struggle of the writer to see his way and
keep his soul alive in this terrific generation. If taken, then, for what it was in-
tended, it may be worth the reading to
some other who is finding this a difficult
time in which to think, believe, and live.
At least, in this hope, it has been written.

HARRY EMERSON FOSDICK.

September 1, 1917.

THE CHALLENGE OF THE PRESENT CRISIS

I

The first question to be answered by any individual or by any social group,

The real handle to a difficult situation

facing a hazardous situation, is whether the crisis is to be met as a challenge to strength or as an occasion for despair. Henry Fawcett, a young Englishman, hunting with his father, suffered an accident staggering enough to break the nerve of ordinary men: his father shot at a partridge, hit his son's eyes, and entirely blinded them. Writing about the matter afterward, young Fawcett said, "I made up my mind inside of ten minutes after the accident to stick to my main purpose as far as in me lay." He kept his word—worked his way through Cambridge University, was made Professor of Political Economy there, was elevated to be Postmaster-General of England, and gave to the British people a generation ago the Parcel Post that we in America have just achieved for ourselves. He took hold of his situation by its real handle; he met it as a challenge to his strength and not as an excuse for disheartenment.

Even a little observation of popular reactions to the Great War reveals many men inwardly looking at the catastrophe in unrelieved dismay. It means to them despair, not challenge. One of the most important battles of this generation is being fought behind closed doors, where men are making up their minds whether this war is to leave them social pessimists or not. While many voices, therefore, are speaking of the significance of the War for political, diplomatic, financial, and military interests, something more ought to be said about the meaning of the War to our personal attitude and faith. All constructive agencies, after the war is over, will depend for their success upon the vision and energy of those who have not been driven by the present catastrophe into cynicism. That many are becoming cynical, are growing dubious of social possibilities, are surrendering to practical skepticism the faith which they never would have surrendered to speculative doubt, is clear to anyone who talks much with men. Materialism as a theory never would have convinced them. But the horrors of Verdun, the mutilated bodies of Belgian boys, the bleaching bones of countless children left by the Russian retreat along the military roads of Poland, and, after sixty generations of Christian opportunity, some five million wounded men in the hospitals of Europe—how shall we keep heart in the face of this?

One natural consequence of such a reaction to the War is a lavish accusation of failure against the ideal agencies on which men had counted to improve the world. As in nervous prostration a man

becomes most fretful against those whom
in normal health he loves best, so, many
people, in the collapse of nerve which the
War has caused, bring the accusation of
futility against the best loved of their
faiths. What most we had relied upon,
seeing that it has not saved us from the
very evil its purpose was to cure, we now
in exasperated disillusionment throw upon
the scrap-heap. Christianity is a failure
—how often has the charge been spoken
and how much oftener has the doubt been
thought!

An initial mistrust as to the wisdom of
this attitude is suggested by the simple
fact that if one is to call Christianity a
failure because it has not forestalled this
war, logically he must box the compass
before he is through and call failures all
those agencies on which we might have
counted to prevent the catastrophe. If
for this reason Christianity is a failure, so
too is education. War may be wicked
from the standpoint of religion, but just
as truly is it foolish from the standpoint

of intelligence, and the universities of Europe and America have been established long enough to have taught men before this the futility of war. If Christianity is a failure because it has not prevented the present disaster, so too is commerce. It promised to bind the dissevered races in an economic unity so close that what happened to one would happen to all, and so to make the race one family. On that interdependence Norman Angell had taught us to rely for the increasing unprofitableness and, as some of us dared hope, the increasing improbability of war. But now the economic bonds are torn asunder; they have proved to be causes of strife, not barriers against it. If anything is a failure, surely that social idealism is, on which we have been priding ourselves these recent decades past. Only a small proportion of those who read these words are likely to be Socialists in a technical sense, and yet all of us had counted on the international Socialist brotherhood, uniting so many million workmen of so many nations in a league pledged explicitly and absolutely against war. Great confidence for the future was begotten when in Berlin's public square 100,000 Socialists at the time of the Agadir incident lifted their hands unanimously against war with France. And yet, in spite of brave attempts, the voice of the Socialists against this cataclysm has been pitiably weak. Christianity a failure? Then surely international law is. The international conventions, guaranteeing the neutrality of Belgium, had expended on them the best brains that statesmanship could supply, but they are scraps of paper now. The leagues and covenants to make the world a more fraternal place, although they are the finest work of our best international lawyers, have been torn to tatters by military necessity. If anything has failed, international law has.

Does any sane man think, however, that it is possible to be content with such a sweeping charge of failure against our ideal agencies? Are they hopelessly to be thrown into the discard? A man who has fallen into a pit might as well saw off his own legs in despite because they did not prevent him from falling in. On second thought, he will do well to keep those legs; they are his only hope of ever climbing out again. His attitude toward them is sadly incomplete if he sits at the pit's bottom, blaspheming the feet that he should have walked straight with. And in the reconstructive age that shall succeed the war, mankind must keep and confidently rely upon those ideal agencies which, with too facile tongues, some folk call failures. Education, fraternalized commerce, social idealism, international law, and Christianity—these are not ready for the discard. They are humanity's great hope. This war is not so much an occasion for despair concerning them as it is a challenge to a better understanding and a finer use of them.

II

If a man, however, with any satisfaction and confidence, is thus to face the

present crisis in terms of challenge, he must have something more than a determination so to face it. Only a frivolous mind can easily be optimistic at a time like this. One who today feels no strain upon his faith has not taken his faith seriously enough to attempt the direct application of it to the actual facts of the war. Let him take his former social hopes into the trenches, the hospitals, the desolated homes of Europe, let him face his old faiths with the elemental human factors that made this war possible and that will make the prevention of its repetition difficult, and he will crave some solid reasons for continued hope, some intelligible justification for accepting the crisis not with dismay, but as a challenge to his courage and devotion.

One intelligible reason for the attitude

which we recommend is to be found in the very factors that make this the most appalling war in history. What conditions necessarily precede the most distressing conflicts that mankind can know? Are they not always conditions of intimate relationship? For this reason the worst of all fights is a family fight. One cannot have a heart-breaking quarrel with a total stranger; there are not points of contact enough. But one can have a dour time in his own family. The very relationships that offer most gracious opportunities for satisfaction, peace, and self-development are the same relationships that offer the most exasperating chance for misunderstanding, discord, and collision. Now, the basic reason for this war's appalling extent and terrific character is that it is waged in a world of increasingly intimate relationships. The ends of the earth have been crowded together as man has conquered distance with his swift inventions. The points of contact between nations

9

and races have been indefinitely multiplied. More than once the telegraph stations around the world have been aligned for a message that made the swift circuit of the globe. Such a message left Oyster Bay one night when Mr. Roosevelt was President. It was a minute later when it went through Denver and a minute later still when it dived out through the Golden Gate. Then it slid past Manila, sang through the Indian Ocean, leaped over the boundary of Asia into Europe, jumped across England, came up from its long bath in the Atlantic on the bleak shores of Newfoundland, and set the telegraph receiver ticking almost before the transmitter had ceased—around the world in nine minutes! A fellowship of life so close and intimate has followed in the wake of these new means of communication that we need not be surprised to learn that when war was declared in Europe food prices in Siam went up 100 per cent. The bullets that fly at the front today fly further than bullets ever went before.

They strike not only the men and boys in the trenches and the women and children at home. They strike the business man in Shanghai and the family with a son of military age in San Francisco; their whirr calls brown and black men from the antipodes and is answered by cannon on the warships of a nation that until a generation ago represented the acme of racial exclusiveness.

Plainly a world of such unprecedented intimacies offers a double chance to its inhabitants. On the one side lies the finest opportunity for racial solidarity and international brotherhood that mankind has ever known; on the other the most abysmal possibilities of friction, collision, and terrific war. Did we really think that mankind was so ideal that dealing with this new situation of multiplied relationships, difficult to handle, full alike of blessing and of curse, it could get all the sweet and none of the bitter? The passions that breed war are deep in the human heart; the traditions that support war are venerable. How could man learn what war would mean in this new world-neighborhood without trying it? How could he handle so new and intricate a situation and not mishandle it? Yet the very conditions that make the consequence of his mishandling so terrible are the same conditions on which are founded our hopes of racial unity and world-wide brotherhood. Say, as we must, that this war in its extent and horror surpasses all its predecessors, yet who would give up the chances of growing internationalism and an ultimate federation of the world that lie in the very intimacies which make the widespread horror possible? The whole course of mankind's increasing interdependence indicates that in this war we are paying the heavy price for the upward climb toward solidarity. We are fighting the war on the way up, not on the way down. Give man time and he yet will learn to handle the new relationships for fraternity and not for war.

Our own American states passed through a colonial period when the points of contact increased beyond the power of wisdom and good will to handle them. The friction of mutual jealousies, impossible between strangers, difficult to avoid between neighbors, issued in tariff wars and even in the invasion of armed bands. At last, within memory of many living, one of the great wars of history was fought before the colliding interests between the states were accommodated in a federation that no misunderstanding ever again will break. Such is the course of social evolution. Those quarrels of the states were met on the way up toward unity. They grew out of the friction of increasing intimacy. Weak men were dismayed at them; courageous men saw the opportunities in the very relationships that were being abused. Today the same problem on a world-wide scale invites the faith and challenges the hope of men. It says: Look *through* the terror of the present hour at the basic elements that make it possible for seven-eighths of mankind to be engaged in the same war. For in the very interdependence of all races and nations lies the possibility of realizing Joseph Cook's dream: "The nineteenth century made the world into a neighborhood; the twentieth century will make it into a brotherhood."

Another reason for accepting this present crisis in terms of challenge rather than dismay lies in the fact that this is the first war in history that has made men widely say that Christianity is a failure. Christendom has not hitherto so perceived the incongruity between war and the Christian Gospel as to feel that the continuance of war was a reflection on Christianity's effectiveness. Some of the early Fathers, to be sure, Tertullian, Cyprian, Lactantius, denounced war as unchristian, but from the time of Constantine the Church and war congenially have lived together. Many of war's worst horrors were alleviated, some of its worst excesses curbed, and the

Church's sanctuaries and truces became oases in the midst of hostility. Always there was a standing disagreement, however latent, between Christ and organized slaughter. But one looks in vain for any such widespread consciousness as we face today that the persistence of war is a staggering blow to the claims of Christianity. Said Athanasius, "It is not permitted to kill; but in war to slay the enemy is both legitimate and worthy of all praise." Said Augustine, "What is the evil in war? Is it that men who are to die anyway die that the victors may live in peace? To complain of this is the part of the timid, not the religious." Said Luther, "War is a business, divine in itself, and as needful and necessary to the world as eating or drinking, or any other work." The popes sent armies out to battle and blessed their banners for the fighting. Henry V's bishops, as Shakespeare rightly pictures them, urged the king to war. And when unbelievers were in

question some Peter the Hermit stormed
Europe with urgent calls to slaughter,
"*Deus vult*"—God wills it. Nor can anyone who listens today fail to hear echoes
of this historic attitude that accepted
war, unconscious of any essential incom-
patibility between the spirit of Christ and
the spirit of a battlefield.

Christianity and war lived in peace together as did Christianity and slavery.
For generations none perceived disharmony between these two. If some now
call the Gospel a failure because war per-
sists, what would they have said if, with
awakened conscience in the matter, they
had lived while Christianity and slavery
walked arm in arm down the centuries?
John Newton, who wrote, "How sweet
the name of Jesus sounds in a believer's
ear!" tells us of blissful seasons of prayer
to Christ, while on slaving expeditions
along the African coast. Cotton Mather,
our own Puritan prophet, thanked God
with full heart for the arrival of a cargo
of slaves and molasses, overdue from the

West Indies, but at last come safely in at
Boston port. Nothing in history seems
to us more essentially unchristian than
the slave raids in Africa, the merciless
conditions of transportation, and the in-
humanities of the slave's life as slavery
spread. Consider a system one of whose
characteristic expressions could be an
advertisement like this, published in our
own country in 1825:

"Twenty dollars reward, — ran away
from the subscriber, on the 14th instant,
a negro girl named Molly. She is 16 or
17 years of age, slim made, lately branded on her left cheek, thus, 'R,' and a
piece is taken off her left ear on the same
side; the same letter is branded on the
inside of both her legs.

ABNER ROSS,

Fairfield District, S. C."

And then consider that one of the last
defenses of that system was written by a
Christian bishop.

But the day came when men began to cry: "Christianity is a failure, it has not stopped slavery." The incongruity between the Gospel of God's Fatherhood on the one side and holding a fellow-being in serfdom on the other, had at last become evident. That was one of the climactic days in history. Aristotle tells us that a few people in his time thought that slavery was unethical. Such occasional insight doubtless had persisted through centuries, a subterranean stream rising in sporadic fountains, some of which we know. But at last the stream emerged fully into the light. Men saw, with regard to slavery, the clear implications of the Gospel; they perceived that Christianity and slavery could not perpetually live together in the same world. The issue was drawn: *Christianity would be a failure if it did not stop slavery.* And from the day that the issue was drawn, the result was assured. It was not Christianity that failed; it was slavery.

When, therefore, men cry today that

18

Christianity is a failure because it has not stopped war, a man of faith may well thank God and take courage.

This, too, is a climactic day in history. For so long time the Gospel and war have lived together in ignoble amity! If at last the disharmony between the spirit of Jesus and the spirit of war is becoming evident, then a great hope has dawned on the race. Only a little while ago many were telling us that Christianity had nothing to do with social questions, that it was a gospel of salvation for the individual out of the wreckage of a ruined world. They urged ministers to "stick to the Gospel" in its application to the separate souls of men and to keep a quiet tongue about the wider applications of Christ's truth. And now we are told that Christianity has failed because it has not stopped war! It is confessed then, that Christianity does have something to do with social questions, that it will be judged and judged rightly not alone by what it does for individuals, but by what it makes of the world in which individuals must live. As for war, the same charge confesses that the issue is drawn between that and the Gospel. Many opinions as to ways and means for bringing permanent security will be entertained, but underneath diversity of method, the main issue is clear: *Christianity will indeed have failed, if it does not stop war.*

If, then, the issue is drawn, this is no time for despair. The situation is a stirring challenge to our strength and our devotion. Impossible to conquer? Rather, as an old reformer cried, "The only difference between the difficult and the impossible is that the impossible takes a little longer time." If mankind had no other outlook than an indefinite recurrence of wars like this, hope for a worthy future for the race would have to be surrendered; stoical fortitude would be our best recourse. But no such disheartened counsel need content us. The conclusion of this world-drama, now at its climax, need no more see the triumph of war than

our fathers' generation saw the triumph
of slavery. If we will, we may have
another victory for Christian ideals.

A further reason for accepting the
present crisis as a challenge lies in the
assurance that comes from the perspective of history. The tremendous events
through which we now are living tend
to preoccupy all our thoughts. We are
obsessed by the immediate, because the
immediate is so absorbingly terrific. But
it is not treachery to the importance of
the present hour to retreat from it far
enough to see it in the perspective of the
centuries. We do not lose faith now when
we read of the Peloponnesian War that
ruined Athens. But contemporaries did.
Euripides' skepticism had for its background that appalling conflict which
brought the pride of his Achaia to the
dust. How modern is his ancient cry!

"When faith overfloweth my mind, God's provi-
        dence all embracing
    Banisheth griefs; but when Doubt whispereth,
    Ah, but to *know!*

21

No clue through the tangle I find, of fate and
of life for my tracing."

We do not lose faith now when we
read of the old barbarian invasions that
devastated Europe, although they over-
threw the civilization on which man's
choicest hopes seemed to depend. But
multitudes of contemporaries did, and
Augustine's "City of God" is the splendid
attempt of a man who would not surrender hope to steady his fellows in the
time of their dismay. The man who
wrote it, aged and unconquered, died
while the victorious barbarians were
hammering at his city's gates. We do
not lose faith now when over against the
French Revolution's fair beginning, prom-
ising liberty, fraternity, equality, we note
its dismal end—the tumbrils rumbling
through the city's streets and the falling
guillotines. But contemporaries had a
bitter struggle to keep heart and Words-
worth in the dismay of the time retreated
to the woods and later described his pain-
ful disillusionment:

THE PRESENT CRISIS

"I lost
All feeling of conviction, and, in fine,
Sick, wearied out with contrarieties,
Yielded up moral questions in despair."

How often have such earthquakes, like the Great War now, thrown the saints upon their faces in dismay! Yet in the retrospect of history, Peloponnesian wars, barbarian invasions, French revolutions take their proper and significant place. They do not now appear as hopeless blockades to human progress. Rather they emerge like rocks around which the advancing stream of the human river swirled for a while and made its progress more evident by the commotion. And in our better hours we know that this present catastrophe so will take its place in history. It is not the end of all things, the finale of our hopes. The unique thing about our generation is not the War. War has always been here. In over 3,000 years of written history since 1496 B. C. there have been hardly more than 227 years of peace. The unique thing about our generation is the way the very people who decide for war, as President Wilson did, are thinking about it. Their obvious abhorrence of war, their increasingly clear insight that whatever may be the necessities of immediate action, war, regarded from the standpoint of the ideal, is the last word in idiocy and infamy as a way of settling international difficulties in the twentieth century—this is more distinctive of our time and country than war itself is. And when a man senses this, he throws aside the despair that in weaker hours confuses him and goes out to do his "bit" for that Divine Purpose in the world, which this war may impede, but which it cannot stop. He determines to play his part, that this war may impede the Divine Purpose as little as possible and that out of it may come indeed a world made "safe for democracy." Behind this attitude he feels the confirmation of history. Ahead of it he sees the promise of hope.

III

If the reader's assent has at all been gained by the reasons which we have *An appreciation of force* noted for accepting the world's crisis as a challenge and not as an occasion for despair, the natural progress of our thought leads us to consider the practical directions which that challenge takes. To us in America the War is now no longer a mere theory to be discussed; it is upon us as a call to action, a stupendous fact whose range and depth of influence no man can measure. Whether or not we should ourselves have voted for America's participation in the struggle, the War is ours now, and its challenge to our Christianity is unescapable. To what does it summon us?

As Christians we are summoned, for one thing, amid all the obsessing influences of war, to keep a clear insight into the limitations of force as an agency in human life. This does not mean that

25

force can be dispensed with. Indeed, since the whole temper of our thought is so anti-militaristic, we may well take special pains to do justice to force, to grant it all the value that its usefulness deserves. Those who put force on one side and love upon the other, as though there were between them an unavoidable antipathy, are creating one of those false dilemmas which are a common stumbling-block to useful thinking. Force and love are not necessarily antithetical. Doubtless it is the absolute ideal that children should be reared by moral suasion only, without compulsion. But because most of us were not absolutely ideal children, we are thankful that we were not reared on an absolutely ideal schedule. We are glad that some things not otherwise obtainable in us were helped by the judicious application of force in the hands of love. Love in its high reaches is not a soft and cooing thing—it is life's most searching and tremendous power, and neither in the family nor in the commonwealth ought it so to delight in the comfort of tenderness that it refuses the discipline of force.

The love of Jesus is commonly appealed to by those who would altogether dispense with force. One has only to read the many conflicting interpretations of Jesus' sayings in their application to the questions which this war presents, to see how difficult, if not quite impossible it is, to build with confidence any solution of our special problems on a literal pressing of the texts. The Master never faced in his own experience, never directly considered in his teaching a national problem such as Belgium met when the Prussians crossed the border. To be sure he fraternized with centurions, taking them for granted as unreprovingly as in his parables he took slavery for granted, but no cause can be made out for or against either slavery or war from this natural attitude of his. The fact is that Jesus did not directly face our modern questions about war; they were not his problem, and

27

to press a legalistic interpretation of special texts, as though they were, is a misuse of the gospels.

It is clear, however, that that boundless love of his, which was the center of his life, was no mild and dovelike thing. It had terrific aspects. The love of Jesus looked on Lazarus, lying untended at Dives' gate, and then the love of Jesus looked on Dives, and God have mercy on him after that! The love of Jesus looked on pious Israelites coming up to the Father's temple to pay their tithes and make their offerings of sacrifice, and then the love of Jesus looked upon the hucksters who rang this piety upon their counters for their private gain; and the love of Jesus took a whip of cords and drove them out. Jesus pictures the ideal of life under the figure of a shepherd, and the tender aspects of the shepherd's ministry so captivate our imagination that we would leave the picture with no shadows in it. Not so our Lord. He is under no such soft illusions about life. He follows through his figure

28

till the thief comes, that he "may steal and kill and destroy"; he adds the wolf as well, who if he can "snatcheth them and scattereth them"; and then the shepherd proves his quality—while the hireling flees—by setting to in desperate encounter to protect his sheep. Jesus knew that a true shepherd could not always be a gentle man; at times the call must come for force. The love of Jesus, as we often are reminded, said, "Bless them that curse you, pray for them that despitefully use you"; and that same love of Jesus, looking on the violaters of the poor, also said, "Ye serpents! Ye offspring of vipers! How shall ye escape the judgment of hell?" Love like his does not always speak gently and act gently; love never can speak and act gently with effectiveness unless it has behind it capacious possibilities of moral indignation. Indeed so stern an aspect did the love of Jesus have that the greater problem which the serious interpreter must face and which pacifist writers commonly forget, is not to harmonize the Master's love with so temporal a thing as the use of force for moral ends, but to harmonize it with so prodigious a conception as the word hell—familiar on his lips—even in its most merciful interpretation must connote. "These mine enemies that would not that I should reign over them, bring them hither and slay them before me"—no soft and comfortable soul, afraid of force, put words like that into his picture of the Eternal. Just as in the Master's love there are heights of tenderness and horizons of compassion where even our imaginations cannot reach, so, in the presence of obdurate iniquity, depths of sternness are there that make us quail. We have been too soft in our thought of him; we have remembered the 6th chapter of Matthew's gospel and have forgotten the 23rd; and some of the most egregious misinterpretations of him ever written have but lately come from extreme pacifists, identifying love with gentleness.

While, therefore, none can be dogmatically sure what Jesus would say about our duty in this present war—although we can be sure that Jesus would hate war and all that makes it possible—one does not see how a soul who spoke as Jesus spoke could forbid as intrinsically wrong the use of force for moral ends. And if, in answer the familiar text is pleaded, "Resist not evil," surely both the context and the whole temper of the Master's life make clear that the meaning there is not passive acquiescence in iniquity, but rather that magnanimity of spirit which Paul summed up in his parallel word: "Recompense to no man evil for evil." For force in Jesus' thought must always be wielded with a heart of love behind and a purpose of good will ahead.

Those who would dispense with force, who at a stroke would lift all opposition to evil from the physical to the moral plane, and fight iniquity with reason and love alone, do not estimate aright what sin can do to human life. They have an

unsupported confidence that no heart ever
grows so callous in iniquity that it is un-
responsive to the appeal of tenderness.
Such folk should go to court some day
when the little children and the fathers
who have beaten them are brought in.
If anything in heaven above or on the
earth beneath can love and forgive beyond limit it is a little child. And these
children have so forgiven and so loved
again the brutal men whose rage has been
vented on their defenseless bodies. Yet
forgiven repeatedly by these little ones,
beset by the appeals of their own children's unconquerable love for them, these
men have gone on beating the scarred
bodies of their own offspring with obdurate cruelty. Sin can work that result
and does work it in human hearts. This
is the deep damnation of sin—that it
makes men's spirits callous until the
nerves are paralyzed that once thrilled to
the touch of tenderness and the appeal of
reason. The state's force cannot save
these men from their brutality—only

love can do that—but it can stop the beating of the children. What do we really think Jesus would have said about it—Jesus who, facing something like it, said it were better for a man, with a mill-stone round his neck, to be flung into the sea, than to offend one of these little ones?

It is true that the advance of society is marked by the progressive substitution of moral suasion for physical force: in wedlock, where men once captured wives and held them by brute strength, but now woo them instead; in parenthood, where a father's power of death over a child was once constraining and where now force is a last resort; in education, where no longer is the birch the tree of knowledge; in penology, where physical compulsion gives way before more generous treatment of the criminal— everywhere the advance of social life involves the gradual displacement of brutal constraint by reasonable persuasion. But this advance of humanity will not bring us utterly past the need of force until it has eliminated more of sin than as yet has gone out of us. Any day on any street any man of us may face an exigency where sin is expressing itself in forms that far have overpassed the power of reason and gentleness immediately to handle. We must use force. The wolf has come and we must be shepherds and not hirelings.

It sometimes is maintained that even in international relations no emergency ever arises which a peaceful good will cannot meet. Writes an enthusiastic pacifist, "Suppose half of Belgium's sons who were killed in battle had died instead as unarmed martyrs resisting German progress, but not to the point of bloodshed—could even the Prussian host have advanced?" To which the answer seems sufficiently obvious: of course they could have advanced, just as they swept through unresisting and now enslaved, Luxemburg; advanced, if there were any determined opposition, as the old Romans

34

slaughtered the unresisting Jews on Sab- /
bath days when the Jews died rather than
fight. One admires those ancient He-
brews, but it is their loyalty to principle
that he admires and not their intelligence.
No more fallacious reading of history is
possible than that which represents the
peaceful peoples as safe from aggression.
The fact is that there never yet has been
an agricultural civilization that grew rich
in prosperity and weak in power that did
not become victim to some predacious
military nation. The gradual substitution of moral for physical force in international relations is as certain as human
progress, for there can be no assured human progress without it, but mankind is
not yet so free from elemental sin that
any nation can count on spiritual sweet-
ness as a safeguard against rampant greed.
Even Jesus did not bless the peaceful; he
blessed the peace-makers; and peace-
making in any human relationship may
any day involve resort to force.

When such exigencies come, no man

can be sure how far the use of force may
have to go. To say that we may use
force up to the point of killing and not
beyond is in practice often an impossible
distinction. It is here that the crucial
difficulty and horror of the Christian
arise, alike in personal experiences where
he has taken life to protect another and
in the frank and brutal slaughter of a
war. Only a few question the rectitude
of parental compulsion or the wisdom of
having our police. The difficulty comes
when the use of force involves killing.
Personality is for Christians the one absolute value in the world, and to push the
use of force to the point where it kills
seems blatant denial of all that Christians
say about the worth of persons. To believe that a man is a son of God and your
brother and yet to kill him—in what fla-
grant contradiction do those two things
stand!

Facing this issue some Christians,
notably the Quakers, have framed their
answer in uncompromising idealism. I

will not kill, says such a Christian. Under no circumstances, even when my own existence is at stake, or a woman's honor or a child's life is concerned, or moral principles are involved that I confess to be of essential value to mankind, will I ever kill. In personal relations I will never so oppose evil as to run any risk of ending the physical existence of anybody, and as for war, I will have no part in it. The nation may jail me, my friends desert me, and public opinion call me traitor, but I will not fight. The business of war is killing men, and to that business I will not consent, in it I will have no share. The enemy may be ruthless beyond reach of the immediate persuasions of reason and good will; he may burn our cities, rape our women, mutilate our children— but I will not kill. Personality is sacred and my hand shall never violate it.

Thus some Christians have spoken and no one who rightly measures the contrast between the Cross of Christ and screwing a bayonet into a fellow-man will lightly scorn their spirit. But this is not the only way in which a Christian may speak. I, too, count personality supremely sacred—so another Christian may say—but *personality and physical existence are not identical.* They are not identical in myself. My personality is God's most sacred trust to me; it is the thing I am, my soul, and to gain the whole world and lose that were a poor bargain; but any day I must be ready to surrender my physical existence for another's welfare and for the ideals that make us men. What is true of me is true of others. Their personality is one thing; their physical existence is another. Any day the exigency may arise where, with no depreciation whatsoever of my estimate of personality's absolute, unrivaled worth, I may, for a woman's safety or a child's life, have to strip some man's physical existence from him, if I can, and trust God that in the world unseen his abiding personality may be recovered from his sin. Nothing is worth more than

38

personality, but many things are worth
more than physical existence, whether
mine or another's, and when the race for-
gets that, the days of moral grandeur are
ended and the doom of heroism come.
Therefore, when other measures fail, I
shall not hesitate to throw my life, at any
risk to my body or to his, against one
who assails what should be inviolate, nor
shall I ever call the Belgians iniquitous
because they risked their own physical
existence and the invaders' in a magnificent endeavor, in the face of perfidy, to
keep their word. Bayonets do not reach
as far as personality; they reach only
physical existence, and the problem of
personality passes far beyond an earthly
battlefield. So a man may speak and
be a Christian.

If such a willingness upon a Christian's
part to risk his own and others' lives in
physical encounter, when rampant evil
resists other cure, seems a compromise
with his ideals, it is only such a compromise as is involved in all endeavor to live

for ideals amid unideal conditions. War is unchristian, but so is our economic system with its terrific inequities. Our economic competition is the war perpetual that runs through all the days of so-called peace and is one of the major causes of that more obvious war that uses sword and shrapnel. No one who deeply sees the evils that our fight for wealth brings on man, with an incidence more terrible than war because it is so continuous and unrelieved, can call it Christian. War brutalizes men? So does our economic system, ruining multitudes with hours of labor that no life can endure, under conditions that no character can sustain. War kills men? So does our economic system, resisting the expense of safer conditions of labor, blowing men up needlessly in mines, pulverizing them in unguarded machinery, poisoning them every day with deadly gases, and on our American railroads running up a death-rate that no necessity ever can excuse. War ruins childhood? So does our economic system, using up children like grist in our mills, and withstanding by every means that money can buy and legal talent can suggest all movements for their relief. There are brave and unselfish aspects to our commercial life as there are to war, and noble men are engaged in both, but no one who knows the under side of our fight for money can help knowing the horror of it. There is hardly a kind of agony on a modern battlefield that has not its counterpart somewhere in our economic struggle.

Shall a man say, then, that because the economic system is unchristian he will have none of it? He could say that if he were in earnest about absolutely uncompromised ideals. He could sell his stocks and bonds, give up his position, refuse to buy and sell, and as a non-resistant pacifist willingly suffers any loss rather than share directly or indirectly in a war, so he could go out alone to live as a monk, free from the entanglements of an unchristian business world.

41

But that man would be shouldering off on others the necessity of dealing with life's stern, forbidding problems and would be retreating into a spiritual vacuum to nurse his absolute ideals. Such an attitude is rank individualism and is obviously unethical. No more can we play the recluse in the face of such a war as this, content to say that fighting is unchristian and that we will have none of it. The answer to such an attitude need involve no defense of war. From the standpoint of every high ideal, war is unchristian—essentially, hideously unchristian. After a look at Europe, let no man ever again speak of a Christian war! The Christian's definite and unrelenting hostility to that international paganism from which war inevitably comes, we shall deal with later. But if, in the present stage of human society, moral values are at stake which ruthless violence attacks, we cannot remain outside the critical problem thus thrust upon us as though we lived in another and a better world. We must help to meet the crisis, with all its wretched necessities, as sharers in a mutual responsibility which no one rightly may evade. To do anything else is to shoulder off on others the burden of meeting life's harsh and unideal emergencies. It may even mean that we sit safely in the lee of the men who use massed force against massed force for righteousness' sake, not because they like to do it but because it has to be done, and that we credit what is really our ignoble individualism with being a fine service of ideals. A noted English pacifist said to the writer that in the present estate of the world he judged that England could have done nothing else in 1914 save to go to war, but that as for himself, he was a conscientious objector and would have no part in it. He acknowledged a social necessity, in the meeting of which he refused any share. Nothing could be more immoral. For, however heartily we may hate the emergencies that the evil of the world presents, we must stay within the problem of

43

international entanglements, as we stay within the economic system, to play our part as best we can in the redemption of both. As a great English Christian put it: "The War presents to every creature whose country is involved in it the one great moral issue of our times and for a man to say he can do *nothing* in it is to vote himself out of the moral world."

Even "conscientious objectors"—rather, they especially and most of all—should face this truth. As the Quakers luminously have shown, a man may be unalterably averse to fighting and yet may take more than a negative attitude toward war. Forbidden by their scruples to engage in war, how often have they stopped the mouths of their traducers by their active, sacrificial contribution to the cause for which others fought! Since they came into existence, every war waged around a moral issue has felt the weight of their support. Sometimes, as in Whittier's day, the Quaker's blazing indignation against moral wrong has fed

the flames of the conflict. Sometimes, as
in England now, the most hazardous
enterprises that the war could furnish,
like sweeping the seas for mines, have
specially attracted the Quaker volunteers.
In many wars their money has gone
where they could not and they have
outbraved the brave in deeds of mercy on
the battlefield. They shouldered what
part they could of the common burden;
they acknowledged their share in the
social emergency; they could not fight,
but they revealed in ways as perilous as
battle their unspoiled conviction that
some things are worth fighting for. One
does not need to agree with such a Quaker's program in order to honor his spirit.
Today he points the only way of self-
respect for a "conscientious objector."
The first business of any man whose
scruples will not let him fight is to find
a post of danger and sacrifice in the common cause that will save him from the
deadly sin of shirking.

As for the Christian who believes that

when force is ruthlessly employed for wrong, it may have to be met by force employed for right, the present war must come to him with a call for service clear and undeniable. He surely cannot thrust on others the meeting of the crisis, while he escapes. He must bear his part, and in those hours when he carries up to God the sad and tangled confusion of the world's affairs, and seeks in the divine light the clue of duty through the labyrinth of conflicting rights and wrongs, he may plead America's cause in sincere and hearty prayer:

O God, bless our Country! We lament before Thee the cruel necessity of war. But what could we do? Our dead by hundreds lie beneath the sea; the liberties that our sires baptized with their blood and handed down to us in trust, so that they are not ours alone but all humanity's, are torn in shreds; and a foe is loose against us whom we have not chosen, whom we have not aggrieved, and who in his will to conquer counts solemn oaths to be but scraps of paper and the chivalry of the seas an empty name. We have grown weary, to the sickness of our souls, sitting comfortably here, while others pour their blood like water forth for those things which alone can make this earth a decent place for man to live upon. What could we do? With all the evils of our nation's life, that we acknowledge and confess with shame, we yet plead before Thee that we have not wanted war, that we hate no man, that we covet no nation's possessions, that we have nothing for ourselves to gain from war, unless it be a clear conscience and a better earth for all the nations to live and grow in. We plead before Thee that if patience and good will could have won the day, we gladly should have chosen them, and patience long since would have had her perfect work. And now we lay our hand upon our sword. Since we must draw it, O God, help us to play the man and to do our part in teaching ruthlessness once for all what it means to wake the sleeping lion of humanity's conscience.

IV

We have endeavored to do justice to the use of force as an agency in human life. *The limitations of force* But the peril with most Americans is not that they will undervalue force during these days of war; the peril is that they will be obsessed by it. In war the instruments with which men endeavor to achieve their ends are instruments of force; and in the thought of our generation what guns and battleships and submarines and aeroplanes and the massed strength of charging men, armed to the teeth, can do is dominant. We Christians need chiefly to be reminded of what these things cannot do; we are challenged to an unremitting emphasis upon the limitations of force, and its futility for all the higher ends of human life. War, like all use of physical compulsion, is at its best a surgical operation. By surgery you may restrain an alien growth, but surgery never cures. The positive, constructive

48

forces of health must cure and without
them surgery is a cruel failure. So war
at its best can do one thing and one
thing only. It can halt some external
work of evil, it can blow away, as in the
American Revolution, oppressive conditions that thwart free development. But
that is all. Its work is all negative, elim-
inative. The agencies of positive health
in social life are not akin to war; they are
good will and friendship and cooperation.
Only these can cure any social ill and
without them the work of the knife is a
bitter failure.

Suppose that the dearest hopes of our
military leaders were fulfilled and that
Germany were conquered by force of
arms until she must confess it and abide
by such terms as we and our allies chose
to impose, what after all would be ac-
complished? We could compel Germany
physically to vacate violated territory;
we could compel Germany to pay indem-
nity, we could cripple the piratical schemes
of pan-Germanism—such things we could

do by force, and leaving it there, would thrust under the ashes of Germany's failure embers of undying hatred that in a generation would flare up again in fire. We would cure nothing. War by itself never cures anything. Mankind is fortunate if war even restrains the evil it was meant to halt and does not create new evils worse than those attacked, as surgery sometimes scatters the cancerous poison that it tries to cut away. But even when a war does the restraining work to which it sets itself, it can cure no radical social wrong or offer to humanity a single solid hope. Only good will can do that. We Christians need to say this to ourselves until it makes the circuit of our blood and comes back to our hearts again. The knife of the surgeon is cutting in; can we supply the constructive forces of social health to make the operation worth while?

We need to say this to ourselves emphatically because whatever may be the fine ideals with which a nation enters

war, as President Wilson phrased them
for us in his noble message, hate thrives
in war-time like germs in a congenial
medium. We have heard much about the
cult of hatred in Germany; we have
cringed at Lissauer's "Hymn of Hate"
against England. But such a spirit is
not peculiarly indigenous in Germany.
Here is Henri de Regnier's song of hate
from France:

"I swear to cherish in my heart this hate
  Till my last heart-throb wanes;
So may the sacred venom of my blood
  Mingle and charge my veins!

May there pass never from my darkened
      brow
  The furrows hate has worn!
May they plough deeper in my flesh, to
      mark
  The outrage I have borne!

By towns in flames, by my fair fields laid
      waste,
  By hostages undone,
By cries of murdered women and of babes,
  By each dead warrior son, . . .

51

I take my oath of hatred and of wrath
  Before God, and before
The holy waters of the Marne and Aisne,
  Still ruddy with French gore;

And fix my eyes upon immortal Rheims,
  Burning from nave to porch,
Lest I forget, lest I forget who lit
  The sacrilegious torch!"

One quotes this not chiefly to condemn it, but to note how natural it is, how spontaneously it rises from the mood that war creates, how certainly we shall be tempted to it in America. Whatever conceivable good this war might possibly do will be undone by such a spirit. If that mood prevails, and in the settlement of the war is dominant, then the war is all sheer waste, a mad expenditure of blood and tears and treasure, with nothing to show for it save graves and poverty and broken hearts and bitter rancor and a world grown worse, not better. For our own sakes and for the world's sake, though we fight we must not hate. We are Christians. We know when we think of it that had we been born in Germany, there is not one chance in a million that we would be doing other than the Germans do. We know that had we been the inheritors of the Prussian tradition, the pupils from early childhood of the Prussian instruction, and the instinctive patriots that all good men are, we should be thinking what the Germans think today. Underneath they are not different men and women from ourselves, and they can no more be conquered in the inner citadel of their hearts by force alone than could we. We never really surrender to anything but good will. Neither will they. Force is evidently the necessary prelude to that capitulation. There is no hope for the world with an autocratic, military Germany triumphant. *We must win the war.* But we must keep ourselves unembittered; we must fight all bitter policies in our government; our good will must be unwearying and strong. We must be as ready to forgive as is God. And in those secret hours when we carry

the tragedy of this war before the throne
of God we must pray for more than our
country; we must pray for our enemies:

O God, bless Germany! At war with
her people, we hate them not at all, and
underneath the cruel divisions that force
on us this sorry business of mutual de-
struction we acknowledge before Thee
those underlying unities that yet will be
there and will be beautiful when war is
over. Our enemies, too, are sons of God
and brothers for whose sake Christ died.
We acknowledge before Thee our part in
the world's iniquity that rolls this burden on Thy heart and crucifies the Son
of God afresh. We dare not stand in
Thy sight and accuse Germany as though
she alone were guilty of our international
disgrace. We all are guilty. We confess
with shame that the present horror is the
natural fruit of sins in which we all have
shared. We beseech Thee against those
things in Germany and in us that make
war possible. And especially we lift up
our prayer for every good impulse in
every German heart, for all misgivings
among Germany's people that cast doubt
upon the policies of frightfulness and ter-

ror, for all the forces of a forward-look-
ing democracy within her, and for every
German Christian on his knees who is
asking Thee for the dawn of peace and
brotherhood. Save to the great service
of the world, we beseech Thee, the won-
derful qualities of the people whom we
fight; let them not perish from the earth,
burned in retributory fire. We need their
strength to be our admiration and our
help, as it now is our despair. O God,
bring us all, Thy wayward people, to
such a penitence and shame at having
made Thy world by sin so sad a place,
that we may learn brotherhood with that
same diligence which now we give to war.

It is no counsel of perfection to urge
such an attitude. This never can be an
impossible ideal to reach, even in war,
while we have before us the admirable
words of Edith Cavell, as she went out to
execution: "I see now that patriotism
is not enough. I must die without hatred
or bitterness toward anyone."

Especially should those who go to the
front with the army purge their spirits of

all hate. We are constantly reminded
that war brutalizes men; but we often
forget that that depends on the man.
The reactions of soldiers to the influences
of war are as diverse as the response of
people everywhere to life's less strenuous
appeals. Some are ruined by war and
some are redeemed by it to a purity of
devotion and a wealth of sacrificial spirit
they have never known before. Some are
besmirched by war and some are cleansed
by it, consecrating their bodies to chastity
for service's sake. The elders among us
who saw the conflict between the states,
say that some men went into the Civil
War and came out beasts. But some
came back from the sights of suffering
and deeds of horror and sacrifices of sur-
passing heroism more tender and beautiful of spirit and rich in sympathetic
humanity than they had ever been before.
A brave and radiant friend of the writer,
suffering the tragic consequences of in-
fantile paralysis, was addressed in sym-
pathy by an acquaintance who said,

"Affliction does so color the life." "Yes," was the swift answer, "*and I propose to choose the color*." That such an attitude is possible toward war by those who are in the thick of its abominations is plain enough from the testimony of these recent years. Donald Hankey is dead now but he has left an imperishable witness from the midst of the battlefield: "I have seen with the eyes of God. I have seen the naked souls of men, stripped of circumstance. Rank and reputation, wealth and poverty, knowledge and ignorance, manners and uncouthness, these I saw not. I saw the naked souls of men. I saw who were slaves and who were free: who were beasts and who were men: who were contemptible and who honorable. I have seen with the eyes of God. I have seen the vanity of the temporal and the glory of the eternal. I have despised comfort and honored pain. I have understood the victory of the Cross. O Death, where is thy sting? *Nunc dimittis, Domine*."

V

Christians are challenged by this war not only to a recognition of the limitations *The case against militarism* of force and to a spirit of unconquerable good will, but to a ceaseless attack upon the whole system of unchristian international relationships of which war is a natural expression. There is one marked difference between the sudden crisis which calls upon a man to attack a ruffian in the street, and the crisis which issues in war. We have not specially prepared for the former. We have not taken it for granted, expected it, armed for it, and assiduously planned for years to meet it. But in international relationships we count war an integral part of our system. We assume it as an event to be expected, and the nations arm themselves against each other and train themselves to slay each other, reckless of expense, as though war and international relations were inseparable. We scheme with mutual distrust in secret diplomacy, make compacts and leagues to each other's hurt, and act in every way as though a condition of international suspicion, envy, and latent hostility were the normal state of the world. Of course war comes. We shall as easily get peace out of the present, dominant idea of international affairs as we shall get figs from thistles. Christian people are challenged to a definite and unending assault upon this immoral and needless paganism.

Some are still so wedded to the present idea of international relationships that they find even the worst issue of them, war, not only unobjectionable but positively desirable. They still talk of the glory of war. The writer once heard a learned judge, justly famed for legal talent and literary genius, declare that a country needed a war about once in thirty years. As well call in the floods of the Mississippi because incidentally they leave more fertile soil; as well call in the San Francisco fire because it showed the pluck of a brave people and made the building of a greater city possible. There are better ways of accomplishing such results than by disasters. Fire and flood are not glorious; all the glory is in the spirit of mankind which is made of stuff too splendid not to show its mettle even in the worst calamities. And war is not glorious, though oftentimes in war men are.

One who knows what really is happening on European battlefields today and calls war glorious is morally unsound. Says an eye-witness: "Last night, at an officers' mess there was great laughter at the story of one of our men who had spent his last cartridge in defending an attack. 'Hand me down your spade, Mike,' he said; and as six Germans came one by one round the end of a traverse, he split each man's skull open with a deadly blow." That is war. Says a Young Men's Christian Association secretary: "Many times these fingers have reached through the skulls of wounded

men and felt their throbbing brains."
That is war. An officer's letter from the
front reads:

"An enemy mine exploded here a few
days ago and buried our brigade. Many
of the men were killed, but some were
not much hurt; so we dug them out and
used them over again."

Sons of God and brothers of Jesus Christ
—"dug them out and used them over
again"! That is war. Said a group of
German prisoners, as they bared their
gashed forearms, "We were dying with
thirst, we had our choice of doing what
some men do in such a case—drink the
blood of an enemy, or else drink our own.
We are Christians: so we cut our own arms
to get drink." That is war. War is not
the gay color, the rhythmic movement,
the thrilling music of the military parade.
War is not even killing gallantly as
knights once did, matched evenly in
armor and in steed and fighting by the
rules of chivalry. War now is dropping
bombs from aeroplanes and killing women

and children in their beds; it is shooting, by telephonic orders, at an unseen place miles away and slaughtering invisible men; it is murdering innocent travelers on merchant ships with torpedoes from unknown submarines; it is launching clouds of poisoned gas and slaying men with their own breath. War means lying days and nights wounded and alone in No-Man's Land; it means men with jaws gone, eyes gone, limbs gone, minds gone; it means countless bodies of boys tossed into the incinerators that follow in the train of every battle; it means prison camps vicious with the inevitable results of enforced idleness; it means untended wounds and gangrene and the long time it takes to die; it means mothers who look for letters they will never see and wives who wait for voices they will never hear and children who listen for footsteps that will never come. That is war—"Its heroisms are but the glancing sunlight on a sea of blood and tears"—and a man who calls it glorious is mad. And through all these physical horrors runs a horror more appalling still, the persistent debauching and brutalizing of men's souls. One who uses his knowledge and his imagination to perceive in its abominations what war really is, while he might never dream of using Walt Whitman's language, finds it hard to be sorry that the language has been used: "Wars are hellish business—all wars. . . . Any honest man says so—hates war, fighting, blood-letting. I was in the midst of it all—saw war where war was worst—not on the battlefields, no—in the hospitals: there war is worst: there I mixed with it, and now I say God damn the wars—all wars: God damn every war: God damn 'em! God damn 'em!"

The last stand of those who still cling to the old illusion that there is something glorious about war is on the claim that war awakens the heroic qualities in men. To such an indictment as we just have brought against war, a very plausible counter is quite possible. Where is it that the ministers of Christ, so the retort might run, look for their finest illustrations of loyalty and courage and sacrifice? When most they wish to inspire that devotion to moral causes on which the welfare of the world depends, where instinctively do they look for allusions to grip the heart? To war. And what hymns do they sing? "Onward, Christian soldiers, marching as to war"; "The Son of God goes forth to war"; "Soldiers of Christ arise, and gird your armor on." War so inglorious and horrible as you depict? Then why is it the foundation of some of the finest chapters in Scripture, some of the most inspiring hymns, and many of the most appealing passages in preaching?

This question is worth asking and worth answering. The defendants of militarism often catch Christian ears with this appeal. Bernhardi's appalling book, stating the purpose of the German war-party, says that war is Christian because it encourages obedience, devotion, and self-sacrifice. And he is right in saying that war uses these noble qualities in men. Today deeds of heroism are being performed upon the battlefields that, when the war is over, will be recalled and cherished as spiritual treasures for the race's memory. The Prussian ensign who, fatally wounded, gathered the flag he carried to his breast, that falling in death upon it he might hide it from the capture of the enemy, presents what a picture of devotion! Or the French commander, calling for a volunteer for a fatal mission, who saw his own son step out, for an instant looked at him with blanched face, and then sent him forth never to return—where shall one seek for more absolute loyalty? Bernhardi is right in this: the record of war is full of deeds whose nobility the race never can forget.

This fact, however, as Bernhardi and many a milder advocate of militaristic glory do not see, is the basis for the most scathing charge against war. Shall not a man of Christian insight say this in answer? O war, I hate you most of all because you lay your hands upon the finest qualities in human life, qualities that rightly used would make a heaven on earth, and you use them to make a hell on earth instead. You take our spirit of courage and devotion, and instead of letting it be a benediction in the world, you use it to burn cities and sack cathedrals and slay men. You take our loyalty that well used would redeem the world, and you harness it to a movement that inevitably means the rape of women, the murder of children, and the starvation of whole populations. You take our religion, and to help your deadly work you rend our God in pieces and make of him a score of tribal deities to whom men pray, as old barbarians, before our Lord had come, prayed to their idols as the gods of war. You take our science, the fruit of our dedicated intelligence, and you make even of that an effective minister of hate, so that while Napoleon in his wide experience never saw a battle-line over fifteen miles long, we have battle-lines 500 miles long, and death falls from the sky and bursts from the earth and hurtles from unseen ambuscades twenty miles away. This is the deepest charge against you, that you take our noblest powers and prostitute them to destructive ends.

How can Christian people fail to see that they are challenged to a tireless fight against the system of international relationships that makes this gross abuse of noble powers a possibility? Men *are* glorious in war. After a charge a wounded American, who was fighting with the troops in France, exclaimed: "We went over the parapet at five o'clock and I was not hit till nine. They were the greatest four hours of my life." Where was the glory there? In war? No, in the spirit of the man—and that spirit is no specialty of war. Captain Scott had it when he crossed the Antarctic continent; Judson had it when he invaded Burma for Christ; Garrison had it when he launched the campaign for abolition. It is the spirit of adventure, loyalty, self-sacrifice, and scorn of danger. The most enheartening revelation of the war is the clear evidence it gives of how widespread in ordinary people these elemental qualities of manhood are. Clerks, ploughmen, bankers, day-laborers from the streets; lawyers, physicians, ministers from their professions—what prodigies of heroism are they all performing! "Look at those millions of men," a recent writer cries, "every man with his back to his home and his face toward his flag, and meditate on the incredible, immeasurable, unimaginable power of patriotism!" But having a human nature to deal with that has such powers of devotion, cooperation, and tireless energy within it, this is the most colossal crime that the race can commit, to use these splendid qualities for slaughter. What a world could be made here, if they were harnessed to a better cause!

Is there anything impossible to a race with powers like these?

There are many who seriously think that it is impossible to do away with war and the conditions that produce it. They do not call war glorious, but they do call it necessary. They have no faith that humanity can put its bayonets and cannon in the museums where they belong with racks and thumbscrews and the shackles of the slave. And one reason for this skepticism is that Christian people have presented as the cure for international hostilities panaceas so pitiably inadequate that no one who knows the problem could believe in them. We never can cleanse the huge Augean stables of our world-wide armaments and wars by gathering a band of people who will persuade some other people never, under any circumstances, in the face of atrocities however great, to fight. The task before us is too gigantic to be handled by such means. Neither can we greatly help the situation by fervid campaigns for unpreparedness, urging individual nations to disarm. Such negative movements for disarmament are bankrupt. Their failure is not due to any untruth in their main contention that to be prepared for war is to invite war. The old illusion that a great military establishment is an insurance against war has been finally dissipated, let us hope, by the present cataclysm. Large armaments are a certain road to war, and militarism, posing as the angel of peace, is the most feckless and muddle-headed sham in history.

The nations, however, even if they know for certain that armaments mean war, will not individually disarm. In the early days of our Western frontiers men carried six-shooters and were quick on the trigger, not because they were bad men. They were the same men they had been before, unarmed and peaceable in Eastern towns. But they were afraid. In the wild, anarchic life of the frontier there was no social order to guarantee a peaceful man his life and liberty. No community was organized that represented the force of all at the disposal of all for the good of all. How useless to argue with individual men in such a situation, that carrying guns encouraged fighting and that therefore each man should throw his gun away! They may not doubt the abstract proposition, but they keep their guns. They are afraid. Only one measure ever made them disarm. The communal life was organized and the forceful protection of life and liberty was delegated to a social order that policed the towns. Fear was removed, and the arms which once seemed indispensable became a needless burden, an anachronism.

No other hopeful road lies open before the nations. We keep armed because we are afraid. Perhaps that fear is our disgrace, our moral failure to trust the spiritual powers of friendship and good will; but when we so begin to think and are almost ready to repent of dreadnoughts and regiments, Austria strikes Serbia,

Germany devastates Belgium, and all the ancient fears come back again. There is only one road out. *We must have a a federation of the world.* No other solution is great enough to deal with our critical need. The nations today are living on the wild, anarchic frontiers of history, carrying their guns in mutual fear, because there is no league of nations to police the world. The forces of good will and brotherhood that are latent in mankind have no fair opportunity to do their saving work. They are stifled by the apparent necessity of armed distrust. No urgent appeals to the nations one by one to lay aside their armaments will meet with favorable response. No negative proposal of any kind can solve the problem of our divided world. The only solution of international discord is internationalism. Wherever force is needed, the force of all must be put at the disposal of all for the good of all.

Does this federation of the nations seem an impossible ideal? But already a con-

crete proposition that has for its vouchers
the leading statesmen of the world is
framed and offered for our support. To
the principles of the "League to Enforce
Peace" President Wilson has given his
assent; and ex-President Taft, Premier
Lloyd George, ex-Premier Asquith, Mr.
Balfour, Lord Grey, Viscount Bryce, and
Premier Briand have promised their support.[1]

Such a massing of international influence around an endeavor after world-
wide cooperation for the good of mankind
has never been known before. No one
supposes that the task is a light one. Was
it easy even to form a federation of our
American states? No one supposes that
he can foresee the details of the plan, the
steps which one by one across years and

[1] Lloyd George said in a Guildhall speech: "The peace and
security for peace will be that the nations will band themselves together to punish the first peace breaker who comes
out." Said President Wilson in an address to the Senate:
"In every discussion of the peace that must end this war, it
is taken for granted that that peace must be followed by
some definite concert of power, which will make it virtually
impossible that any such catastrophe should ever overwhelm
us again. Every lover of mankind, every sane and thoughtful man, must take that for granted."

centuries will lead to the goal. But this federation of the world not only can be achieved; it must be. All the forces of man's economic and moral life demand that it be done. Better far to live in isolation, each nation behind its Chinese wall, than to come out into our new world-wide intimacies and then not learn the secret of mankind's larger unity that alone can bring peace instead of war. And to this unwearying conflict against our present international paganism in favor of this federation of the world, the Christian people supremely are challenged.

In one essential part of this campaign, the innermost and preeminently essential part of it, the Christian people have unique responsibilities. Behind and around all forms of organization which our statesmen may devise for international cooperation, there must be developed in all the people the *international mind*. Once men of clannish tradition found it hard to think in tribal terms; then men of tribal mold strained their minds to

national dimensions; and now we with
our national sectarianisms find it difficult
to think ourselves citizens of the world.
No scheme of universal policy that state-
craft can devise will work until the people
are internationalists in their thoughts.
And Christianity is challenged by its
Master to give to men that horizon to
their loyalties, that Fatherland for their
sacrifice. If this seems a platitude, it is
one of those platitudes whose most obvious applications have not yet been even
dimly seen by multitudes of Christians.
In 1860 a man in Maryland said, "I am
firstly a citizen of Hartford County;
secondly a citizen of Maryland; thirdly a
citizen of the United States." How
amazingly provincial such words sound a
generation after! One wonders if this
man was a member of a Christian church,
a believer in the Christian creed, a pray-er
to the Christian God. And then he sees
how many churchmen still are like him—
no disciples of Jesus in any deep, intelligent sense. For the Christian's citizen-

ship must always begin at the other end from Hartford County; he is firstly a citizen of the Kingdom of God on earth, a patriot for mankind. A Christianity that is not international has never known its Master.

No fine loyalties in human life, however sacred and essential they may be, are ever ruined, they are glorified by being subjugated to a larger spiritual unity. Jesus did not hurt the family when he said a man should hate his father and mother, his wife and children, if they stood athwart the Kingdom's triumph in the world; he *made* the family. Family life in Christendom has grown beautiful just because it has been subjugated to a spiritual idea and made a moral, not simply a natural relationship. Nationalism will not be hurt by being overpassed in international concord and cooperation. Rather, this alone can ever make nationalism great, can cleanse it from its ignoble strifes and mean ambitions, and can wash patriotism pure from hatred and malignity. As things stand now, patriotism is half curse, half blessing. It runs to chauvinism and sinister designs on other's goods as readily as it does to noble sacrifice. It issues in slaughter as easily as it does in service. Only one thing can save nationalism from its perversions and that is internationalism. Patriotism *needs* to be mastered by a greater unity before it ever can be really great itself. If it is to mean unqualified blessing to the earth— a generous rivalry in service and not a malign consecration of selfishness under a holy name—patriotism must surrender its primacy to a world-wide loyalty, wrought into the habitual thinking of the people and expressed in agencies of international cooperation and goodwill.

To work this inward transfiguration of man's thinking, which alone can give effectiveness to the outward devices of our statesmen, is the task of religion. Nothing but religion is adequate to the task. The words of Dr. Charles E. Jefferson ought to be nailed to the doorposts of every Christian's memory: [1]

"Science cannot kill war, for science has not the new heart, and whets the sword to a sharper edge. Commerce cannot kill war, for commerce lacks the new heart, and lifts the hunger of covetousness to a higher pitch. Progress cannot kill war, for progress has no heart at all, and progress in wrong directions leads us into bottomless quagmires in which we are swallowed up. Law cannot kill war, for law is nothing but a willow withe tied round the arms of humanity, and human nature when aroused snaps all the withes asunder and carries off the gates of Gaza. Education cannot end war, and if by education you mean the sharpening of the intellect, the drawing out of the powers of the mind, the mastering of formulas and laws and dates and facts, education may only fit men to become tenfold more masterful in the awful art of slaughter. Who will end war? The world has had

[1] "What the War is Teaching," pp. 198-199.

three historic scourges: famine, pestilence
and war. Each one numbers its victims
by the tens of millions. Commerce killed
famine. By her railroads and steamships
she killed it. It lies like a dead snake by
the side of the road along which humanity
has marched up to the present day.
Science killed pestilence. The Black
Plague, the Bubonic Plague, Cholera,
Smallpox, Yellow Fever—all have re-
ceived their deathblow. Science did the
work. These foes of mankind lie bleeding
and half dead by the side of the road along
which the world presses on to a higher
day. Who will kill war? Not Commerce
and not Science, nor both of them together. Only Religion can kill war, for
religion alone creates the new heart.
Without religion we are without hope in
this world. Without God we are lost."

VI

If religion has such a part to play in
the program of internationalism, we, as
The challenge Christians, are challenged
to the to a searching examina-
churches tion of our faith and
works, and to a fresh devotion to our
cause. One of the wisest and most pic-
turesque explications of the present crisis
is attributed to Bergson, the French phi-
losopher. He says, in effect, that the chief
work of science has been to enlarge man's
body. Telescopes and microscopes have
increased the power of our eyes; tele-
phones have stretched our hearing to
some three thousand miles; telegraphs
have made our voices sound around the
earth; locomotives and steamship lines,
better than seven-league boots of ancient
fable, have multiplied the speed and power of our feet; and French big guns have
elongated the blows of our fists from two
feet to twenty-five miles. Man never
had such a body since the world began.

THE PRESENT CRISIS

The age of the giants was nothing compared with this. But man's *soul*—there the failure lies. We have not grown spirits great enough to handle our greatened bodies. The splendid new powers which science furnishes are still in the hands of the old sins—greed, selfish ambition, cruelty. The innermost necessity of mankind is a spiritual life adequate to handle our new acquisitions. Some things we can do without, but one thing, in this war, has grown obviously indispensable. We must have a new access of moral vision and power or we are utterly undone.

As a thoughtful Christian stands before this challenge he must repent, for himself and for the churches, the lamentable inadequacy of our organized religion to meet the crucial need. Were it not for such institutions as the Young Men's and the Young Women's Christian Associations, and the Federal Council of the Churches of Christ, we should have to cover our faces in confusion. This war will fail of one of its most beneficent

81

results if it does not drive the sense of shame into the Christian churches with a poignancy that no excuses can palliate. In the presence of a gigantic task, calling for a federated Church, we stand a split, dissevered flock of churches. In the presence of abysmal need, demanding a great religion of comprehensive faith and devoted social spirit, we stand—how often! —tithing "mint and anise and cummin," and neglecting "the weightier matters of the law." We are challenged by this war to a renovation of our popular Christianity, to a deep and unrelenting detestation of the little bigotries, the needless divisions, the petty obscurantisms that so deeply curse our churches, to a new experience and a more intelligent expression of vital fellowship with God. Unless we can answer that challenge, there is small use in our trying to answer any other. We must have a great religion to meet a great need.

The saddest aspect of Christian history is the misrepresentation of Christ and the

spoiling of his influence, not by irreligious
men but by the official exponents of religion. The belittling of religion by its
devotees is the most tragic narrative of
Christendom. The unhappy story began
with the Master's earthly ministry. As
he emerged among a people where the
minute disputes of rabbis were so large
a part of piety, how great in contrast was
religion as it appeared to him! It meant
to him an inward fellowship with God so
close that to tell where he left off and God
began is like discerning the air's fragrance
from the sunlight on a radiant day. It
meant to him a thought of God that sent
him out to the help of men with a love
no sin could turn aside and no ingratitude
could quench, and with a hope that shone
for him on desperate days like a beacon
from below the line of the horizon, ad-
vertising from afar that the haven was at
hand. And after all these centuries, with
what an ample sweep do the truths move
that his religion meant to him! The
Fatherhood of God, the brotherhood of

man, the friendship of the Spirit, the inexorableness of moral law, the supremacy of the Cross, the campaign for the Kingdom, the life eternal—what weight and range must the words have that try to tell what his faith meant to him!

And coming so to men, with his great religion, what opposition did the Master meet that most perplexed and disconcerted him? He faced bad men like the Prodigal, but with a love and hopefulness that never failed and never were dismayed. He found selfish men, like Zacchæus, but he refused to let their meanness blind his eyes to their possibilities. But another type of men he met, that he could not understand and against whose obdurate life his spirit spent itself in vain. These were the religious men who discussed whether it was the will of God that men eat eggs which had been laid on the Sabbath Day; and one school said it was and another said it wasn't. These were the religious men who by a ritual word escaped their moral obligations to their parents or stood in the temple thanking God that they had fasted twice a week. Only one type of man, our Master, with all the wide ranges of his pity and compassion, could not understand—the religious man who belittled religion into technicalities and reduced the service of the living God from ethics to etiquette. How the Master's spirit chafed against these! "Ye blind guides," he said, and there was agony in the cry, "that strain out the gnat and swallow the camel!"

A thoughtful Christian cannot fail to see that when our Lord comes now to us, in the crisis of this terrific war, he finds us too, with our petty emphasis on the technicalities of sectarian religion, poorly prepared to understand the spiritual greatness of his message, unready to interpret it to a world, whose footsteps, lacking it, have manifestly taken hold on ruin. Many a man among us, reared in some special sect, as he now recalls the preaching that he has heard remem-

bers how much of it concerned the minu-
tiæ of the sect. At times he almost was
constrained to think that only where
he stood was holy ground, and he
alone with his few fellow-devotees elect
of God. So Ruskin tells us that he gave
up his evangelical faith because a sermon
that he heard at Turin was the last
straw: "A little squeaking idiot," Ruskin writes, "was preaching to an audience
of seventeen old women and three louts
that they were the only children of God in
Turin; and that all the people outside the
chapel and that all the people in the world
out of sight of Monte Viso, would be
damned."

But as our Christian grew he saw how
certainly religion was greater than his
sect. The very hymnals unconsciously
advertised the fact. For even in his little
church, he sang with a Methodist, "Jesus,
Lover of my soul," and with an Episco-
palian, "Rock of ages, cleft for me,"
and with a Congregationalist, "I love
Thy Kingdom, Lord," and with a Presby-

terian, "Jesus and shall it ever be, a mortal man ashamed of Thee," and with a Unitarian, "In the cross of Christ I glory," and with a Roman Catholic, "Lead, Kindly Light," and with a Baptist, "Blest be the tie that binds our hearts in Christian love."

Surely religion was greater than his sect. Still when he thought of folks, not Christians, who never had heard of Christ, unnumbered millions far and wide around the world, the majority of the children of God, he grouped them under one word— "heathen." Then some things that the heathen did began to disturb his soft complacency. He found that some heathen in India pray like this:
"O Lord

> From the unreal lead me to the real,
> From darkness lead me to light,
> From death lead me to immortality."

He found that some heathen in China pray like this:

> "Spirits and men rejoice together, praising
> God the Lord. What limit, what measure

can there be, while we celebrate his great
name? Forever he setteth fast the high
heavens and shapeth the solid earth. His
government is everlasting. His poor
servant, I bow my head and lay it in the
dust bathed in his grace and glory."

If our Christian was wise, he did not
from this conclude that all religions are
equally true and good. A man may not
here abdicate the first work of intellect,
which is discrimination. Buddhism, Con-
fucianism, and Christianity represent
quite distinct philosophies of the spiritual
life and can no more be equally true than
can contrasting hypotheses in science. But
with the outward sweep of his horizons he
did begin to see how much greater a thing
religion is than he had used to think, how
deep its fountains lie in human souls,
how unescapable is the spirit's thirst, like
the homing instinct of the bird, for the
God from whom it comes. He did begin
to see that as love is in human life, so is,
religion; that in forms low or high all men
know them both; that low they curse

men, and high, bless them with ineffable benediction. And in hours of vision when he saw it so, and heard the deep in man calling out for the deep in the Eternal, it seemed to him that he was coming close to the heart of Christ, close to the springs of his exhaustless passion to reveal the living God, without whom man cannot be really man.

When one in such a spirit comes to the religious world today to work in it and through it, a jargon pitched in an alien key astonishes his ears. "You cannot sit at my communion table," one sect is saying; "Nor you at mine," another cries. "Your rituals are inexact, your ordinances are incorrectly understood." He sees strange sights—in 1890, 137 different kinds of Christians in the United States, now 165. And if he listens from within, what bickering over details of polity, what petty pressing of legalistic texts, what endless splits twixt Tweedle-dee and Tweedledum—as though our Lord would not once more, if he were here, wither with blistering scorn such rabbinical belittling of the faith! Are these times that seem to call for such minute finesse? As one thinks of the world today, shaken in an earthquake that brings clattering down about our ears the dearest dreams our hearts have cherished, it does seem that religion should grow great to meet her crisis and opportunity, and casting aside the littleness that in calmer days might find excuse, ought to speak great words about God and the Kingdom, lest men's hearts turn to water in them and their strength be gone. This is the challenge of the present crisis to the Christians. The New Testament does not say that "Every knee shall bow and every tongue confess" that our church or our theology alone is true. The New Testament says that "Every knee shall bow and every tongue confess that Jesus Christ is Lord." If we were large enough so to interpret him that men could see him as he is, unperverted by our littleness, they soon would understand his claim to spiritual mastery. "Our Father, who art in heaven, hallowed be thy name"; "Thou shalt love the Lord thy God, with all thy heart and with all thy soul and with all thy strength and with all thy mind, and thy neighbor as thyself"; "By this shall all men know that ye are my disciples, if ye have love one for another"; "Thy Kingdom come, thy will be done on earth as it is in heaven"—is there anything local or provincial about words like those? Are they not as broad, as deep, as high as human need? And are not his disciples challenged to labor unceasingly for such a generous freedom of opinion on details, such a dominant emphasis on the central message of the Gospel, and such a fraternal federation of the churches for united work, as will make the need of the world the opportunity of Christ to come to his own?

The practical need of this is made vivid in an unexampled way by the world's disaster. The nations are forever striving to avoid war when it is too late; they try to dam the stream after the spring freshet has begun. The only way to guard against war, so far as war arises from the embittered passions of the people, is by constructive campaigns of good will, launched long before the first rumbling of a coming conflict. What now is our surest reliance in America against any unresolvable misunderstanding with China? It lies in the $10,000,000 which out of sheer good will our government returned to China when the Boxer indemnity was paid. Hundreds of Chinese students supported by the interest of that fund are studying in America now, and in every intelligent Chinese mind there is a settled predisposition to trust America.

We have just adopted a gigantic budget of $7,000,000,000 for the purposes of war. How magnificent—and how pathetic! Consider what a very little of that prodigious sum would do if, instead of being voted after war begins, it were appropri-

ated before war was thought of for such
international service as the Boxer Indem-
nity Fund is furnishing. Utopian? On
the contrary the most sane and eco-
nomical statesmanship! To spend billions
for the means of slaughter when millions
previously expended in good will for service would often make the means of
slaughter needless, is folly so supreme as
almost to justify the saying that soldiers
often fight, not for their country but for
some blockhead of a diplomat. The cost
of that folly we loyally will pay, and our
children after us will be paying it for
generations; but, as Christians, we may
not be silent about the folly itself nor
cease our unwearying antagonism to it.
So few times in history has any nation
done what America did for China, and so
overwhelming is the response to such
simple friendliness that the nations cannot permanently be blind to the good
sense, as well as the ethical nobility, of
such a course. The extreme pacifists
insist that there is no situation which

kindness cannot handle. They are wrong
if they mean that kindness can begin at
any time, appealing to the Prussians,
for example, after the assault on Belgium
has been started. But they are right if
they mean that kindness begun soon
enough and practiced long enough in the
end will prove omnipotent. We yet shall
learn that the best armament of any
people is the friendship of the world, won
by constructive good will.

The application of this truth to the
churches' missionary program is manifest.
The cause of missions has too often been
presented in its significance for individuals
alone; it has been pictured only as the
snatching of souls one by one from ruin.
But this crisis in the world's life challenges
us to balance our view of missions with a
more social concept of their meaning.
*The missionary enterprise is the Christian
campaign for international good will.* We
must see that it is so and must handle it
as though it were so. What the nations,
through their governments, will slowly

learn to do, loath to leave old precedents, bound by the sectarian narrowness of national loyalties, Christians must do now, and do with a lavish generosity that they have not practiced hitherto.

We are told that some day we shall have war with Mexico. How much our own fault it will be if such a lamentable conflict comes! What Mexico needs is an invasion of school teachers and social workers and Christian preachers, who have caught the idea of missions in their international relationships; and if such an invasion is not forthcoming, a military invasion may indeed be necessary. One suspects in many a case like this that we have our choice. We are continually reminded of clashing interests that some day will embroil us with Japan. Even the present war could hardly be a more grievous catastrophe than that. And short of some league of nations which may offer means of mediation and settlement not today existent the surest hope of avoiding conflict, of forestalling war by friendship, is an energetic campaign of good will now. If the Christians of America do not want war with Japan, they need not have it. Japan is not mad enough to want war with America. Only we must begin now, under the leadership of Christian missionaries and statesmen like Dr. John R. Mott and Dr. Sidney Gulick, a determined movement within our country against our needlessly insulting legislation, when Orientals are concerned, and we must organize such expressions of good will through our missionary agencies that, if possible, we may create a predisposition in the Japanese people to believe the best of us and not the worst. The missionary enterprise at its very heart is the impulse to share our finest, and if the finest in America and the finest in Japan were thoroughly known to each other, the chances of collision would be minimized to vanishing. Such a ministry of mutual interpretation and reconciliation is committed to the churches. The present war is an appalling commentary upon our failure to fulfil or even to acknowledge our obligations. We have seen our duty in too little terms; we have but dimly understood what the Master wanted of us. We are challenged to understand it now; the call is written in lines of fire on the map of the world; and we shall be renegade, indeed, if we do not now accept before it is too late the opportunity for international service which this war reveals.

Such is the challenge of the present crisis. We have talked of it as though its appeal were directed to the nations and the churches. But we shall not deal fairly with the world's appalling need if we fail as individuals to hear the call it sounds for each of us. A writer in the *Atlantic*, to whom Good Friday, 1917, with its sacred memories and its imminent entrance of America into the war, came with overwhelming solemnity, has issued a call that no one can honorably deny: "The greatness of the whole nation is so inextricably bound up with its individuals that I beg again each one of you now to say to himself or herself, 'This means *me*. It means me and *my* life, *my* best self, *my* highest ideals, if the magnificent opportunities of the times are to be realized.'"

There may have been other days when selfishness could find excuse in the smooth ease of the nation's prosperity, but the last shred of such excuse has been torn now from every selfish undedicated life. An American visitor at the French front was allowed a three hours' conference with Marshal Joffre. He has said, in the writer's presence, that the most impressive incident of the conversation came when the Marshal drew from an inner pocket a well-worn letter, written by a French mother to her son in Canada, and, with unsteady voice, read this:

"MY DEAR BOY:

"You will be grieved to learn that your two brothers have been killed. Their country needed them and they gave everything they had to save her. Your country needs you, and while I am not going to suggest that you return to fight for France, if you do not return at once, *never* come."

Multitudes are living in that spirit today. He must have a callous soul who can pass through times like these and not hear a voice, whose call a man must answer, or else lose his soul. Your country needs *you*. The Kingdom of God on earth needs *you*. The Cause of Christ is hard bestead and righteousness is having a heavy battle in the earth—they need *you*.